YES YOU CAN

KNOW THE REAL YOU

ANAMIKA RAI

/ BookLeaf
Publishing

India | USA | UK

Dedication

*I DEDICATE THIS BOOK TO
ALL WOMEN OUT THERE
WHO WANTS TO LIVE LIFE ON
THEIR OWN TERMS AND
READY TO SACRIFICE
WHATEVER IT TAKES. THE
ONES WHO DARE TO EVOLVE
AS THEIR TRUE AUTHENTIC
SELF.
THIS BOOK IS FOR WOMEN
WHO DO NOT WANT TO LOOK
FOR VALIDATION FROM
ANYONE AND BE THEIR OWN
BIGGEST SUPPORTER .*

Preface

*THIS COLLECTION DEPICTS JOURNEY OF
WOMEN AND WOULD RE-SURFACE MANY
UNSAID EMOTIONS & STRUGGLES. IT
BRINGS FOCUS ON THE UP BRINGING &
CONDITIONING OF WOMEN BY SOCIETY
FROM THE DAY SHE IS BORN .
WHILE SHE IS TAUGHT TO PRIORTIZE
OTHERS OVER HER OWN HAPPINESS &
SACRIFICING HER DREAMS TO SUPPORT
HER DEAR ONES, SHE IS NEVER TAUGHT TO
RECOGNIZE THE POWER WITH IN .*

*A SHOUTOUT TO ALL WOMEN OUT THERE,
WHO ARE YET TO REALISE THEIR TRUE
POTENTIAL*

Acknowledgements

I offer my sincerest gratitude, to the divine for the journey he has destined for me and people who have been part of this journey in all forms. A sincere thanks to BOOKLEAF PUBLISHERS for giving this beautiful oppurtunity to NEW POETS, to be able to bring their creative work in front of everyone, from comfort of their homes.

1. BROKEN SOUL

Broken into the finest manner,
That it has become quiet,

Lying on the ground all scattered,
Has began to love the lying,

Do not make me move now,
Moving will make the noise,

Started to love the silence now,
Just let me be by my side,

Broken into the finest manner,
That it has become now quiet.

2. LET ME FLY

Do not stop me, let me fly
Do not dictate your believes and limitations on me
Let me be the one ,to decide for mine

Yes you gave birth, raise me up
But by your believes and limitations
please do not dim my shine

You had your chance to dare, dream and to be the shine
Do not stop me because you believe, I am not the one
meant to shine
You may have your strengths, believes and limitations
But I realized, they are not mine

When I was borne, the world around
Assumed me to be the one who was to make others
shine
So I believed and supported others , for a very long time
Yes it took me long to know my strength
And now when I know, I decide to fly

Do not dictate your believes and limitations on me
Let me be the one , to decide for mine.

3.

Do not stop me, let me fly
Do not dictate your believes and limitations on me
Let me be the one ,to decide for mine

Yes you gave birth, raise me up
but by your believes and limitations
please do not dim my shine

You had your chance to dare, dream and to be the shine
Do not stop me because you believe i am not the one
meant to shine
You may have your strenghts, believes and limitations
But i realised they are not mine

When i was borne, the world around ,
assumed me to be the one who was to make others
shine
So I believed and supported others , for a very long time
Yes it took me long to know my strength and now when
i know,

i decide to fly

Do not dictate your believes and limitations on me
let me be the one , to decide for mine

3. WHAT YOU CHOOSE TO BE?

You have been raised as a good girl
The one, who is trained to obey
No questions asked, no answers to be seeked
Just do as you are told to and then you are a good girl

Your existence should not threaten mine,
You should not challenge the intellect i outshine,

What skills, why skills, do not ask for something that
makes you shine
Because if you do , the societal norms for you to get
married will be not as defined
So what if you are capable of being independent, may be
you have the strength but will not let you threaten mine,

So I decide to dim your shine & you let me do as you are
a good girl

*I know you deserve better but i cannot let you be the one
who is unconventional & undefined
It makes me feel less as a gender and you my young one
did something, I never thought you were meant to find
As I never reached there and access was denied, I never
thought you would reach there and shine.*

*Now I feel less though I wanted you to shine but not so
much that I loose mine
I never believed in your strength , as you came through
me
And I was never so strong to fight
So I close my eyes and decide not be there to say that
I am proud that you outshined*

*To comfort thyself, I name it as luck
But imposed my beliefs to your life even when you
outshined*

*So girl what you choose to be, please decide
To be a good girl or you want to outshine*

*I urge you to sharpen your strength, intellect, desire or
dare to dream
And lighten up the human intellect that is meant to
shine.
The path will not be easy, as it has to be walked alone*

So ask yourself
Do you dare to pay the price?
What you choose to be ?please decide
You want to be a good girl or an intellect that is meant to
shine

3.

You have been raised as a good girl
The one who is trained to obey
No questions asked, no answers to be seeked
Just do as you are told to and then you are a good girl

Your existence should not threaten mine,
You should not challenge the intellect i outshine,

What skills, why skills, do not ask for something that
makes you shine
Because if you do , the societal norms for you to get
married will be not as defined
So what if you are capable of being independent, may be
you have the strength but will not let you threaten
mine,

So i decide to dim your shine , i decide to dim your
shine

I know you deserve better but i cannot go to some one
who is above mine
It makes me feel less as a gender and you my young one
did something, i never thought you were meant to find
As i never reached there and access was denied, i never
thought you would reach there and shine.

Now i feel less though i wanted you to shine but not so
much that i loose my shine
I never believed in your strength , as you came through
me
And i was never so strong to fight
So i close my eyes and decide not be there to say that
I am proud that you outshined

To comfort thyself, i named it as luck
But imposed my beliefs to your life even when you
outshined

So girl what you choose to be, please decide
To be a good girl or you want to shine

I urge you to sharpen your strength, intellect, desire or
dare to dream
And lighten up the human intellect that is meant to
shine.
The path will not be easy, as it has to be walked alone

So ask yourself
Do you dare to pay the price?
What you choose to be ?please decide
You want to be a good girl or an intellect that is meant to
shine

4. YOU MATTER

Smile because you matter,
Do what you feel is right because you do matter,
The very presence of you in this world matters
No one can be you and you do matter,
Experiences you gathered and lessons you learned are
yours
and they do matter
Realize your strength and share your struggles
because they do matter

The path you walked may become the light for the soul
somewhere out there
yet struggling to fight
You sacrificed you for those who mattered to you
but did you asked them do you matter?

No one will come and say to you that what you do ,
matter
Stand for your self, know your strength,
Tell your self first that you do matter

Please do not wonder, if tomorrow your loved ones do
not see that you matter.
the show will go on, you stay or go
So before its too late
Love your self and say you matter
Smile because you do matter

5. THE JOURNEY WAS DESTINED........

Yes i often smile, to hide all the times i wanted to cry
Times that were moments of pain, hurt,
disappointments, struggles and fights
It was put on my path and i was supposed to rise

To rise, be bright and yet to be right, for the path i was
destined
But what is this path?, i often ask divine!!!
The path and purpose for which, i am being made
Not only to survive ,but also being right

Faced it all many a times, asked my self am i paying the
price
Price for being kind , soft and always ready to be nice
It hit me hard, my own heart and soul was made to fight

The mistake i realised ,yes i was kind but forgot to
protect what was truly mine

Doing all the things i sacrificed for the ones!!!!!!!!! i thought to be mine

6. THE HOPE & DIVINE

Amidst the darkness also, I always had you.

Giving me hope and faith, telling i am there for you
Watching me, guiding me, giving me strength
To move through the storms, I designed for you

I do not know whether to complain, get angry , fight to
you or say thank you
For all the growth i gained while fighting the storms, you
put me through

You raised me up from ashes, removed the fears i
thought i was not strong enough to go through
Now i am not scared to walk amidst the storm
Because i know i always have you.

7. A FRESH MORNING

Says keep moving and smiling,
Neah, i am not saying everything will be fine,
But keep your charm and spirit alive,
So when you step outside, every problem you meet ,
makes you shine

Do not get troubled and loose your shine
Remove the glasses of reactive emotions
And you will again see the sun shine

A fresh morning says , there will always be a way
No matter what you go through, you will still be alive

8. MOTHERHOOD

In every heartbeat, I feel you near,
A gentle whisper, banishing my fear.

With every stumble, you taught me grace,
In your embrace, I found my place.

Through sleepless nights, your lullabies sung,
In the tapestry of love, our souls are spun.

You light my darkest days, a beacon bright,
In your laughter, I find pure delight.

Together we journey, hand in hand,
In this beautiful chaos, we forever stand.

Your dreams entwined with mine, they soar,
In your spirit, I see forevermore.

So I'll hold you close, and never let go,
For in loving you, I've learned to grow.

You are my heart, my reason, my song,
In this world of ours, where we both belong.

DEDICATED TO MY SON

9. AN UNTOLD STORY

Standing still, do not know where to go
Want to stay, but forced to go
Love is there but scared to share now
Trust is broken and so the soul deep down
An untold story,
Standing still do not know where to go
Yet hope flickers, a soft golden glow
In the silence, I find strength to grow

10. SILENCE

Silence has its own power and is also a language of
desire
Be with someone , who knows the difference
You are silenced, to comfort others fire
Break it when desired
Should know what it is you want to hold
Not every expression is required, but know when its
becomes a fire that burns your own desire

11. THE NEW ME

The old me, who cared, vanished somewhere
It stayed for quiet long, believe me before it died
It cared a lot, valued others over self
Gave too many explanations, even when the fault was
not mine
To secure relations, even self respect was sacrificed

Holding my sensitive and innocent soul ,so tight
For this cold world, I was not strong enough to survive
Got betrayed, manipulated and lied
Was always made to felt, that the fault was mine

Got myself broken to the worst, that i could survive
And that is how my old self died
Believe me , It stayed quiet long before it died

Now here i am , the one that is ready to take the fight
No explanations, seeking validations or crying through
nights
Bring it on now, i am all set to fight

12. DREAMS & DESIRES

Dreams & desires, what is it that you really chase?.
Desires change, as you achieve one, you want to be more
Based on the fantasies , they make you run
Chase is on and it never goes

It may take you away from the real you
Influenced by family and friends near you
Do remember their journey are not yours
So know your self and be bold
Focus on one that makes you stronger
The real dreams once achieved will not make you further
want more
focus your emotions on goals and not on some fantasy
you want more and more

13. LOVE

Embrace the quiet moments, let them heal
Whisper secrets to the stars, let your soul feel

Every scar tells a story, every tear a sigh
Hold yourself gently, as the night passes by
For those who learn to thrive in their solitude
Find a deeper connection, a blossoming gratitude

Let the winds of self-acceptance guide your way
With every step forward, let your heart sway
Forge a bond with your essence, let it be known
That the greatest love story is the one that you've grown.

14. THE BEAUTY WITH IN

Oh! being a woman, you were taught beauty is the thing
a woman has got ,
Never taught to be more, the value was placed in this all
Conditioned by own people and the world around
At the end, this is the aspect where your value will be
found
So constantly groomed, to look for validation from
people you surround
Was it your fault, that you were not taught to love self &
depend on the people around

Conscious is sleeping, all are walking around
Doing, Believing and Acting the way it has been existing
around

Let the mirror reflect strength, let hearts break their
mold,
To embrace every story, let their truths be bold.
Whispers of worth hidden beneath layers of doubt,
Ignite your inner fire, let the voices shout.

Oh, shine in your essence, let the world see your glow,
For beauty's not one-sided; it's the wisdom we sow.
Reclaiming our stories, our laughter and tears,
Embracing the struggles, confronting our fears.
For in unity's strength, we stand hand in hand,
Creating a sisterhood, a resilient band.

15. SHAKTI

You worship shakti & She is the one
But are you ready to foster that strength and fire, she
holds within
When she is borne, You often hold desire of more.
Denying the truth , the one you worship and the one
borne has the same fire
You are worried with the ideas of protecting her and
Summing up the money .
She becomes a responsibility and not something to be
seen as fire

To the human form,
Yes you made her empowered
But yet you believe she needs someone to protect that
fire
And not someone , who has the power to raise a life.

16. REFLECTION

When was the last, you saw yourself in the mirror
When was it you did something for your self
You got raised, trained and tamed , prepared to fulfill all
the roles

But you were never told to put yourself first and give to
yourself
The one who had the onus of raising you up, never loved
their ownself
How the wisdom would have been passed to you
Please awaken the real you, know you and become
something you were told you can never be

Go to the mirror , not to see your outer reflections
For this you have been told and trained enough
Go within, take the journey and see your inner self
Because it is only when you believe in you, others will
Otherwise the chase for constant validation , will never
let you survive

17. CRITICIZE - YOU MAKE ME WISE

You criticize & I obliged
The circus goes on, till I decide to fight
When I fight, I am made to pay the price

When I want to keep it straight, then I am made to walk
the path, not so easy to ride
To avoid the nuisance, if I become quite
Then I am tagged , being not so socialite
Oh !! yes I am selective , and that is my right

You invest your time on me, to criticize
I am thankful, you are making me right
I see the attention in your noise
And I appreciate you, for all the criticism you provide

Grateful to all the critics out there
You make me , what I am today
I will not exist , if you do not make noise!!!!!

18. WALK ALONE

Do not be scared, walk alone
Have the courage to choose your path , even if without
support
Yes you gave it all and it still not worked
At times you have to let go, what you desired the most

Invest in you, your dreams and desires
Under any condition, keep burning your fire
Your fire is the one , that keeps you alive
Your survival never depended on support and validation
you thought was desired

You may or may not get what you desire
But have the courage to walk alone
And believe in your fire

www.ingramcontent.com/pod-product-compliance
Lightning Source LLC
Chambersburg PA
CBHW050959030426
42339CB00007B/409